Lucky

Lucky

Symbols of good fortune from around the world

Megan McKean

Hardie Grant

BOOKS

Contents

Introduction   07

Acorn   08
Albatross   10
Amber   12
Carp Scales   15

Chimney Sweep   16
Coins   19
Cornicello   20
Crescent Moon   22
Cricket   24
Crocodile Teeth   27
Dala Horse   28
Dice   31
Dolphin   32
Dragonfly   34
Dream Catcher   36
Elephant   39
Evil Eye Talisman   40
Four-Leaf Clover   43
Frog   44
Goldfish   46
Grapes   48
Hamsa   51
Horseshoe   52
Key   55
Lady Beetle   56

Lotus Flower   58
Lucky Bamboo   60
Maneki-Neko   63
Mushroom   64
Number Seven   67
Oranges   68
Pig   70
Polaris   72
Pysanky Egg   75
Rabbit   76
Rainbow   79
Sapphire   80
Scarab Beetle   82
Seashell   84
Shooting Star   87
Snail   88
Sparrow   91
Swallow   92
Tiger   94
Tortoise & Turtle   96
Tortoiseshell Cat   99

White Heather   100
Wishbone   103
Wishing Well   104
Wreath   106

About the Author   110

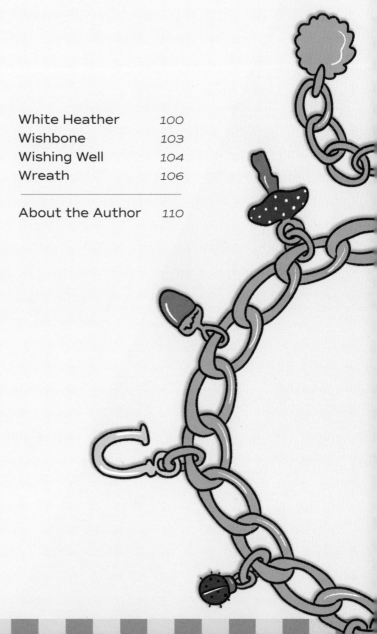

Introduction

Luck is chance; it is a personal success or failure brought about by happenstance. The word 'luck' likely comes from the Dutch word *luc*, meaning 'happiness' and 'good fortune'. The desire to feel in control of life events has led people to create rituals to influence luck – for both protection from the bad, and to harness the good.

Lucky charms span centuries, cultures and countries. These physical amulets and talismans are believed to hold good fortune within them, wielding positive effects. Beliefs about luck have been shaped by superstition, folklore, tradition and religion, and as a result many different tokens, symbols, colours and numbers are believed to be lucky today.

Research has shown that believing in good luck can boost optimism and confidence, which leads to increased enthusiasm and perseverance, and ultimately success. Hold onto a charm or two as you go about your day, and you might just find yourself feeling a little more lucky.

Acorn

In Norse mythology, oak trees were believed to be sacred to Thor, a god associated with thunder and lightning. Strong enough to withstand wild storms and lightning strikes, the oak tree represented protection and prosperity.

The protective powers of the mighty oak could also be found in its fruit – the acorn. The tiny nut was placed on windowsills as a gesture of respect to Thor and to safeguard the home from lightning.

While the oak tree symbolises longevity and endurance, the acorn symbolises potential and growth. From these little things, big things can grow.

Albatross

The albatross, a revered symbol of maritime folklore, was believed to possess magical qualities of protection and guidance; its ability to fly extraordinarily long distances is considered a sign of supernatural power. Because of this, it was a good omen if an albatross followed a boat, as the bird was thought to provide safe passage for the seafarers through the wild waters and back to land.

This symbol of good fortune has also come to represent an unwanted burden. In the eighteenth century poem *The Rime of the Ancient Mariner*, the narrator kills an albatross at sea, bringing death and despair to the sailors. He is made to wear the albatross as a display of shame – this is the origin of the phrase 'an albatross around my neck'.

Amber

Wearing the badge of 'luckiest gemstone that isn't even a stone', amber is a fossilised resin long thought to possess mystical properties. Scandinavian Vikings revered amber as the tears of Freyja, the goddess of love and beauty, and carved pieces of stone into various animal shapes. They believed that each carving contained the individual strengths of that animal species.

Roman gladiators carried pieces of amber into battle, trusting their stones would offer them protection and courage. Today, amber symbolises the sun's energy; in crystal healing the warm yellow stone is thought to release positivity, acting like a personal sunny day for the holder.

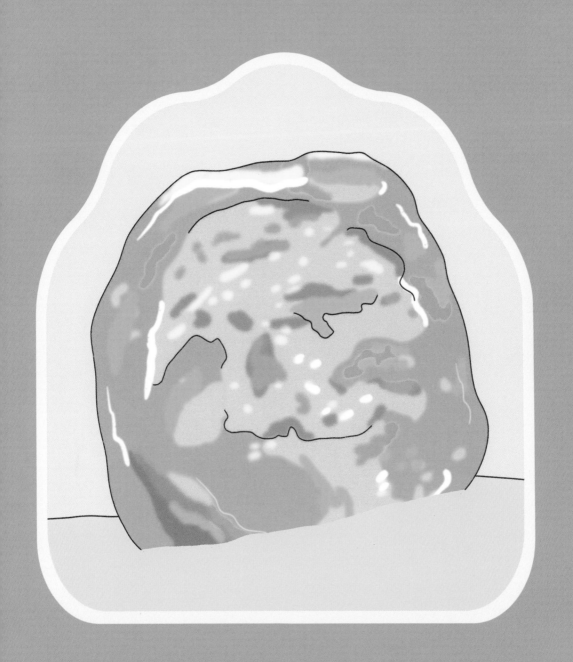

Carp Scales

Eating carp on Christmas Eve is a popular tradition
across several Eastern European countries, as is
looking for any scales left on the table after the
meal. Collecting the scales and keeping them in your
purse or wallet for the following twelve months
is said to bring you wealth for the year ahead.

In Poland, carp has been considered a fish fit for
kings since the twelfth century, with the most
famous fish farms breeding what's known as 'royal
carp'. This connection to royalty is believed to have
contributed to the superstition that keeping
the fish's scales will attract riches.

Chimney Sweep

Good luck by royal decree! Such is the positive symbolism of the chimney sweep across Europe and the United Kingdom. It's said that sometime in the 1700s, England's King George II was riding in a procession through London when his horse was spooked by a growling dog. The horse became out of control, causing the king to lose his grip on the reins. A local chimney sweep calmed the horse, dashing forward to save King George – and earning a lucky reputation for the profession from that day forward.

So grateful was the king that he declared that all chimney sweeps were a symbol of future success and should be treated with respect.

Coins

More than just currency, coins have long been
connected to luck and superstitions. In Ancient
Rome it was believed that finding a coin with the side
showing the emperor's face was a sign of good fortune.
The common rhyme 'See a penny, pick it up, all day long
you'll have good luck' echoes this belief today.

Millions of coins are thrown into Rome's Trevi Fountain
each year, tossed into the water by hopeful visitors.
Legend has it that one coin thrown into the fountain
means you will return to Rome, while two coins will lead
to romance and three coins to marriage.

Many cultures use coins as 'touch pieces': small tokens
believed to cure disease and bring good luck. Keeping
a penny or small coin in a pocket or wallet will bring
good fortune to the bearer.

Cornicello

The *cornicello* (Italian for 'little horn') is a symbol of good luck and hope. Sometimes called the *corno portafortuna* – 'the horn that brings luck' – Italians have been wearing the cornicello since the Neolithic period, an era when animal horns were considered to be symbols of strength and good fortune.

Reminiscent of a chilli pepper, the cornicello is sometimes hung from the rear-view mirrors of cars and inside houses, though it is most commonly worn as jewellery.

It is also said to repel the *malocchio*, a superstitious circumstance characterised by negative energy and envy, similar to the evil eye.

Crescent Moon

In Greek mythology, Selene was the goddess of the moon, said to drive her chariots of white horses across the sky, giving light to the night. The Roman goddess Diana is often pictured with a moon, as is the Hindu deity Shiva, who bears a crescent moon on his head.

A symbol of transition and change, the crescent moon is worn to bring wealth and good luck, and in some cultures to protect against misfortune. It was a popular motif in Victorian jewellery, often paired with stars, the combination of celestial symbols representing guidance and clear direction.

Cricket

By Jiminy, listen to those crickets chirp! As long ago as 500 BCE, people kept crickets in cages to enjoy the song that they create by rubbing their wings together. Farmers would time their harvest to the song of a cricket, the chirps indicating cold weather on the way. The cricket's ability to jump is said to offer the power to leap over a difficult situation.

Charles Dickens even titled one of his novels *A Cricket on the Hearth*, believing 'to find a cricket on the hearth is the luckiest thing of all'. Following this, it was popular to keep a brass cricket by the fireside to ward off bad luck.

Crocodile Teeth

Crocodile teeth strung around the neck
is more than just a bold fashion statement
– it's also thought to bring good luck when it
comes to matters of money. A popular token
among gamblers, crocodile teeth are the
charm used to attract wealth.

The crocodile's ability to latch onto and
keep hold of its prey in its strong jaws has
seen it become a symbol of power and
perseverance, a representation with its
origins in Haitian voodoo.

Dala Horse

An unofficial symbol of Sweden, the brightly painted Dala (or Dalecarlian) horse is a common fixture in many homes and souvenir stores around its home country. Originating in Dalarna in central Sweden, the Dala horse was once a simple wooden toy, carved and painted using traditional techniques. It was an item of great value and linked with good fortune due to the skill involved in its creation.

In 1939 a giant Dala horse was displayed at the New York World's Fair, and from that time it became known as a good luck charm the world over. In the year following the exhibition, more than 20,000 horses were shipped all over the world to people wanting a little more luck in their lives.

Dice

While the origin of the numbered dice remains largely unknown, cultures around the world have used animal knucklebones and rocks as a form of dice for millennia, for gambling, games and fortune-telling. Today, blowing on dice before casting them is said to give a boost of luck to gamblers.

During World War II, pilots would place lucky trinkets in their planes as talismans for their safety – usually poker chips and dice. They believed that if these charms could bring money, they could offer protection too. After the war, the connection between decorative dice and good luck continued as a tradition thanks to the rise of 1950s car culture, this time transformed into a pair of fuzzy dice suspended from the rear-view mirror.

Dolphin

Long considered lucky by seafarers, the dolphin is
seen as a helper and protector in many cultures and
mythologies. Poseidon, the ancient Greek god of the
sea, had a particular fondness for dolphins and even
had a dolphin lieutenant named Delphin. Poseidon is
said to have created the constellation Delphinus for
him, a timeless honour written in the stars.

When sailors spent months at sea, they took the
sight of dolphins swimming next to their ship as a
sign that land was close by. Dolphins are considered
a good omen and are often used as a lucky charm
for a safe journey.

Dragonfly

With its iridescent wings and body in shimmering jewel tones, the dragonfly has been an object of fascination for centuries.

Fishermen believed dragonflies to be a sign of good luck, trusting that wherever the dragonfly hovered, there were plenty of fish to be caught. If a dragonfly landed on an individual, they would have great fortune in their life.

In Japanese culture, the dragonfly is a symbol of courage, adorning swords and arrow quivers of soldiers in the seventeeth century to bring strength and protection.

Dream Catcher

The dream catcher is a Native American amulet,
originating thousands of years ago in North America.
A wooden hoop with a woven web made of string,
it is often adorned with feathers and beads.
The woven strings signify a spider web, able
to catch whatever lands within it.

Commonly hung by the bed, and always near a
window, a dream catcher will let the night's good
dreams flow through the web but catch the bad
ones. As dawn breaks and sunlight touches the
dream catcher, the bad dreams evaporate, leaving
the sleeping owner well rested and refreshed
for the day ahead.

Elephant

The belief that elephants are lucky has its origins in Indian and South-East Asian cultures, where the elephant is revered in the Hindu and Buddhist religions. They are associated with the elephant-headed Ganesha, the god of wealth and prosperity.

American culture appropriated the elephant as a good luck charm following World War II. Soldiers returning from the war brought home with them knowledge of Asian culture, and media attention focused on the rare white elephants owned by Thailand's royal family as sacred symbols of royal power.

There is also a superstition that an elephant with its trunk pointed upwards means you will be 'showered with luck'.

Evil Eye Talisman

A well-known symbol of protection, the ancient
talisman that protects against the evil eye
is especially prominent throughout the countries
of the Mediterranean and West Asia. In Arabic this
charm is known as a *nazar*. The evil eye is usually
a curse cast by the malicious glare of someone
wishing misfortune on another.

The evil eye talisman is traditionally designed
in the shape of an eye, and coloured blue or green
to foster spiritual protection and so act as a shield
against evil. It is often worn as jewellery or a small
accessory. As well as warding off negative energy,
it brings good luck to the wearer.

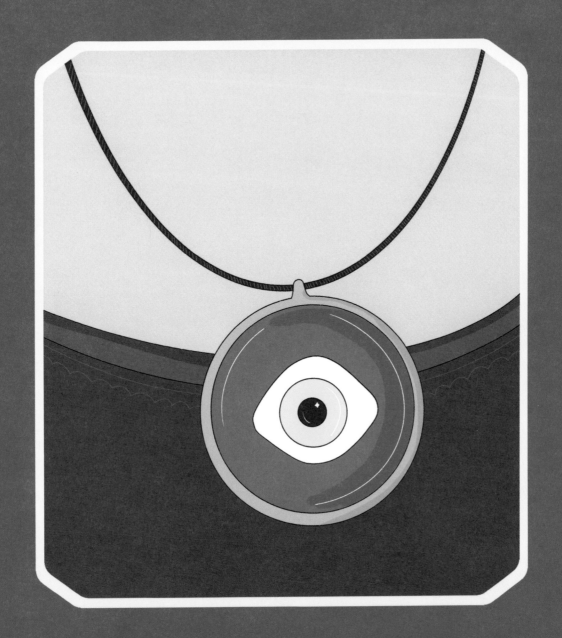

Four-Leaf Clover

According to legend, Eve plucked a four-leaf clover as a souvenir when she and Adam were evicted from the Garden of Eden. This connection to the foundation story of several religions has meant that the four-leaf clover has been considered lucky ever since. Some folk traditions assign a different attribute to each of the four leaves: hope, faith, love and, of course, luck. It's said that four-leaf clovers are most commonly found in Ireland – which perhaps gave rise to the phrase 'the luck of the Irish'!

While the odds of finding a four-leaf clover are around one in 5000, they occur in clusters, so if you find one, your good fortune will likely occur again.

Frog

The frog has been a symbol of luck in many cultures throughout history, perhaps because if you spot a frog, it means a water source is close by. The ancient Romans linked frogs to the goddess Aphrodite, a symbol of plenty. First Nations Australian, Native American and Vietnamese cultures all connect the frog to abundance and renewal, while Japanese tradition views the amphibian as a lucky charm that will bring a traveller safely home again.

Madrid is home to a giant – albeit outlandish – frog sculpture, a gift to the Spanish city. Carved into the frog's belly are a variety of symbols, including a scarab beetle, clover, horseshoe and dolphin. Luck on luck!

Goldfish

During China's Song Dynasty, the domestic breeding of silver carp led to a colour mutation in the fish, resulting in yellow and orange scales. Yellow carp were forbidden to be kept by anyone other than the royal family, so commoners kept the orange version, giving them the name 'goldfish'. Their golden colour linked them to wealth and good fortune, and they quickly became popular pets, often given as good-luck gifts, especially during Chinese New Year.

Goldfish are said to attract luck and tranquillity. It was once a European tradition for married men to gift their wives a goldfish on their first anniversary, symbolising many prosperous years of marriage ahead.

Grapes

The Spanish tradition of *las doce uvas de la suerte* or 'the twelve grapes of luck' consists of eating twelve grapes at the stroke of midnight on 31 December. Popularised in the early 1900s – it perhaps originated with Spanish grape growers encouraging sales after a particularly abundant harvest – it continues to be followed today as a fun tradition to welcome the new year.

With each grape representing one of the coming twelve months, they are eaten one by one on each of the twelve strokes of midnight. If you can finish the full dozen before the last toll fades, it's believed you will have a luck-filled year.

Hamsa

The *hamsa* is a hand-shaped amulet, popular throughout North Africa and the Middle East. Archeologists have traced the early use of the design back to ancient Mesopotamia, finding the symbol on jewellery and the walls of buildings made as long ago as 1000 BCE. The word 'hamsa' derives from the Arabic word meaning 'five' or 'five fingers of the hand'.

Commonly associated with themes of prosperity, strength and wisdom, the hamsa will sometimes feature the shape of an eye in the design, which is believed to protect against illness or the misfortune that the evil eye can bring.

Horseshoe

One of the oldest symbols of luck, the horseshoe and its connection to good fortune has many mythologies and superstitious origins. Horseshoes were originally made of iron – a material with magical powers in folklore, believed to ward off evil spirits – and were traditionally affixed to the horse's hoof with seven nails – seven being the luckiest number.

Today they're often nailed above the entrance to a home, bringing good luck to those who enter. Whilst the symbol is widely recognised, opinions remain divided on which way up the horseshoe should be displayed. Ends pointing up, allowing the horseshoe to catch the luck? Or ends pointing down, so the luck pours out of the horseshoe onto those entering the home?

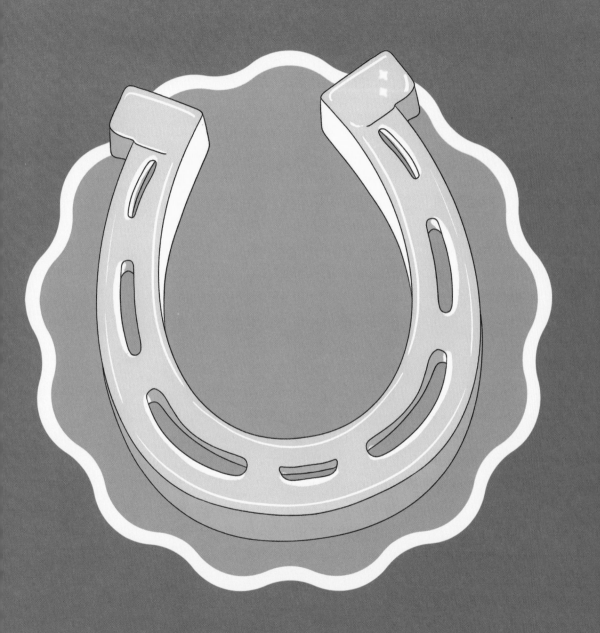

Key

Connected with gateways and doors, keys have long symbolised fresh beginnings and new possibilities. In Christianity, Saint Peter was given the keys to heaven, and Anubis, the ancient Egyptian god of the dead, was frequently depicted with a set of keys to escort departed souls to the underworld. The Hindu god Ganesha is often shown with keys, and locks featuring Ganesha etched onto them represent the passage to knowledge.

Keys symbolise unlocking the unknown, with hopes and dreams existing on the other side of the doors. In Japan, wearing a symbolic combination of three keys is said to encourage the doors to love, health and wealth to open.

Lady Beetle

Luck will be a lady when these little bugs are near!
The daintily dotted red lady beetle was given
its name by farmers who long ago prayed to the
Virgin Mary to ask for protection of their crops.
These insects would eat the pests and were
referred to as 'the beetle of our Lady'; over time
this was shortened to lady beetle ... or ladybug,
or ladybird! Whatever name you know them
by, they are a popular symbol of good fortune
in many cultures around the world.

If a lady beetle lands on you, the number of spots
on the shell is said to predict how many months
of good luck you'll have!

Lotus Flower

An important symbol of Buddhism, the lotus
flower represents the blossoming of the mind
and the spiritual journey of enlightenment.
Lotuses bury their roots in the mud at the bottom
of the pond, then send their shoots up towards
the light, blossoming into flowers on the surface
of the water. Rising from the mud without stains
on their petals, lotus flowers are viewed as symbols
of purity and rebirth.

A lotus placed by a window is thought to invite
peaceful energy into the home, bringing with
it good luck in love and social relationships.

Lucky Bamboo

Lucky bamboo has featured for centuries in feng shui, the ancient Chinese art of creating harmony and balance in an environment. While actually a tropical water lily rather than a true bamboo, this easy-care indoor plant is a symbol of good health and prosperity that will activate stagnant energy in the home.

The plant is a popular gift at times of celebration: for example, it's believed that if you receive it as a New Year's gift you'll have good luck across the coming year. The type of luck heading your way is connected to the number of stalks on the plant, with two said to 'double your luck', three symbolising wealth and happiness, and nine stalks the optimum for overall good luck.

Maneki-Neko

The *maneki-neko*, or beckoning cat, is a well-known symbol of good fortune in Japan. A common sight in homes and businesses, the figurines are said to bring good luck to the owner. These cats – based on the Japanese bobtail breed – are typically depicted seated, holding a koran coin and with one paw raised. When the right paw of the cat is held up, it is believed to bring prosperity.

According to folklore, the Gotoku-ji temple in Tokyo is the birthplace of the maneki-neko. Some time during the Edo period, a feudal lord got caught in a thunderstorm, and a cat beckoned him inside to safety with a waving gesture. Today tourists can visit the shrine and see more than one thousand figures of the cat.

Mushroom

Popping up as if by magic, mushrooms are the
embodiment of an overnight success. They are
often connected with fairies and elves, and
have a fascinating history in the folklore and
mythology of many cultures around the world.

The fly agaric mushroom is a good luck symbol
in German culture; the *Glückspilz* (lucky mushroom)
is especially prominent at Christmas and New Year.
These red-capped toadstools are a common ornament
on German Christmas trees, expressing hope for
positivity in the coming year. The belief that finding
a mushroom in the woods will bring you good fortune
expresses reverence for the forest and the beauty
found in nature.

Number Seven

The number seven is the most popular choice when it comes to lucky numbers, and it's a number found all around us – from the seven colours of the rainbow and the seven notes of a musical scale to *Snow White and the Seven Dwarfs* and the Seven Wonders of the Ancient World.

Many religious beliefs are connected to the number seven: followers of Islam and Judaism believe in seven heavens, and Christians believe God created the world in six days and used the seventh to rest.

Seven will surely be your favourite number when you line up three in a row on a slot machine ... jackpot!

Oranges

Oranges have been a good luck symbol in Asian culture for centuries, associated with prosperity and good fortune. In Chinese, the word for 'orange' sounds similar to the word for 'wealth'.

In many cultures, mandarin oranges are given as gifts during auspicious occasions, such as weddings and New Year celebrations, because they are believed to bring good luck and wealth to those who receive them.

The round shape of the orange is said to symbolise unity and completeness, and the cheerful, bright colour represents joy and happiness.

Pig

For hundreds of years, pigs have been symbolic of wealth and prosperity. Nordic mythology reveres the wild boar as a sacred pet of the gods, and board games from the Middle Ages have given pigs a high value in play. In ancient Greek and Roman cultures, owning pigs denoted privilege and affluence, and the Chinese thought pigs represented wealth and fortune.

Germanic cultures still see the pig as a lucky charm today, with the *Glücksschwein* (lucky pig) given as a gift around New Year's Eve. These days the gift is most often a symbolic replica, often made of marzipan and usually with a penny or four-leaf clover in its mouth for extra luck. In German, 'Schwein gehabt!' ('Got a pig!') is an idiom, the expression meaning 'to be lucky'.

Polaris

The original GPS, Polaris – also known as the
North Star – has been used by explorers for
centuries as a tool for navigation in the Northern
Hemisphere. Before the invention of the compass,
sailors relied on this dependable star – which
appeared to be stationary in the sky throughout the
night – and considered Polaris lucky, as its presence
in the sky meant they were nearing home.

Still a popular symbol today, the North Star
represents staying on course, and receiving
protection and guidance through life.

Pysanky Egg

Eggs represent fertility and rebirth, and symbolise new beginnings. Many cultures and religions associate them with Easter traditions, celebrating with brightly dyed eggs or foil-wrapped versions. It's thought that the eggs celebrate the start of spring, the yellow egg yolk representing the return of sunshine after a long winter.

Pysanky eggs are one of Ukraine's national symbols, their name stemming from the word *pysaty*, which means 'to write'. These Ukrainian Easter eggs feature complex floral and geometric designs, applied with beeswax before the eggs are dyed; there are more than one hundred unique symbolic patterns.

Rabbit

In the Chinese Zodiac, rabbits represent a long life, tranquillity and prosperity. In the United Kingdom, it's believed that saying 'rabbit rabbit' before uttering any other words on the first day of a new month will bring good luck for the next thirty days. The phrase is thought to have originated from the story *Alice's Adventures in Wonderland*, in which the White Rabbit was Alice's guide.

Many cultures around the world believe a rabbit's foot is an amulet that brings good luck. There are many variations of this superstition, and over time the symbol has garnered more and more rules. One legend states that the back left foot is the luckiest.

Rainbow

An awe-inspiring natural phenomenon and a colourful sign of hope, a rainbow in the sky symbolises the chance to start over. Rainbows appear only after rain and harsh weather conditions, and so are commonly associated with renewal and new beginnings, bringing light after darkness and storms. In the Bible, a rainbow appeared after the Great Flood as a promise from God that he would never flood the Earth again.

In Irish folklore, leprechauns guard a pot of gold at the base of the rainbow, symbolising wealth, good luck and achieving one's goals – should you ever make it to the rainbow's end.

Sapphire

The sapphire has been prized as a valuable gemstone since at least 800 BCE. Ancient Persian rulers believed the sky was painted blue by the reflection of sapphire stones. In the Middle Ages, people believed sapphires offered protection against treason and fraud, and royalty frequently wore the stones to protect themselves from harm.

Although sapphires can be found in a variety of colours, they are generally recognised as blue gemstones. The word 'sapphire' stems from the Latin *saphirus*, meaning 'blue'. The more intense the colour, the more valuable the stone. The sapphire is thought to bring luck to many areas of life, such as wealth, joy and fulfilment.

Scarab Beetle

The scarab is one lucky symbol that really gets on a roll!
Originating in ancient Egypt, the beetle-shaped amulet
was a reflection of the heavenly cycle, representing
regeneration and the eternal cycle of birth, life, death
and resurrection. A type of dung beetle, the scarab's
life consists of collecting dung by rolling it into a large
ball – it eats the dung and lays its eggs in it, before
burying the sphere underground as a food supply
for its hatching young.

The Egyptian god Khepri was believed to roll
the morning sun across the sky each day, similar
to the way a scarab beetle rolls its ball of dung.

Seashell

The conch shell is thought to be the original horn, historically used around the world in many cultures and symbolising differing beliefs about the good fortune it holds. Buddhist beliefs see the conch shell as a charm for magic that will bring learning, protection and riches. Conch shells are kept outside the home, never indoors, in order to keep the sea outside.

In feng shui, seashells attract good luck when kept at home, as they are symbols of healthy relationships and prosperity. Keeping shells at the window protects the home from negative energy.

Shooting Star

A shooting star sends a streak of light across the night sky, a captivating sight that lasts mere seconds. Many beliefs and superstitions about shooting stars abound, with some cultures believing that they represent the souls of deceased loved ones who continue to watch over their family and friends from the heavens. Others see them as a sign of a positive change in personal fortune.

The Greek astronomer Ptolemy thought shooting stars signified gods looking down on Earth from above, providing a chance for humans to communicate with them. It's thought that this is where the practice of making a wish upon a star originated, casting one's desires into the air as the meteor falls through the sky.

Snail

The snail creeps into ancient myths and legends from all around the world. In Ireland, it was thought a black snail would be unlucky to meet, whereas a white snail would bring good fortune. These slimy creatures make an appearance in Egyptian hieroglyphics too, the spiral of their shells symbolising consciousness, evolution and the expansion of life.

The Aztec god of the moon, Tecciztecatl, was often depicted with a snail on his back or his head, symbolising the moon and the spiralling of its phases. A European superstition of the 1800s thought that the trail left by a snail before sunrise marked the initial of your true love's name.

Sparrow

In many cultures, the sparrow is believed to bring good luck and is commonly associated with positive signs, such as the presence of love, hope and joy.

In Native American cultures sparrows are seen as a symbol of companionship, and they are mentioned in the Bible as a symbol of God's protection and care. Ancient Egyptians used the symbol of a sparrow to denote 'small' or 'narrow' in hieroglyphics and believed sparrows could help guide the souls of the dead to the afterlife.

In China, if a sparrow flies into the home, it is a sign of good luck, and in Indonesia it can mean someone will find happiness in love.

Swallow

The swallow is symbolic of good fortune in many cultures, and in ancient Greece was associated with the goddess of love, Aphrodite. This bird has a long-held significance for sailors, who tattooed symbols of them on their skin in the hope it would provide safety at sea. In Japan, swallows are known as harbingers of happiness. As the cherry blossoms begin to bloom, swallows make their way to Japan, where their arrival is considered a sign that spring has begun.

Swallows are loyal to their nesting sites, often returning to the same location year on year. Having a swallow's nest on your property is thought to be good luck for your home, and the swallow's annual return illustrates faithfulness and devotion.

Tiger

The tiger is known as the king of all beasts in China, and throughout history has been a powerful emblem of protection and great strength. A symbol of luck, courage and protection in many Asian cultures, they have a deep connection to folklore, with numerous gods in Hindu and Chinese mythology depicted riding tigers.

As well as bringing good luck, it was believed that tigers had the power to chase away forces of evil, and a tiger image would often be carved into tombs to symbolise protection.

Tortoise & Turtle

The tortoise is one of China's Four Auspicious Beasts, the revered guardians of feng shui. Its hard shell and lifespan of up to 150 years make it easy to see why it symbolises protection and longevity. The tortoise is often attributed with wisdom and great patience; Aesop's fable *The Tortoise and the Hare* illustrates the virtues of moving towards a goal – no matter how slow or difficult the journey.

In Hawaiian culture, a turtle – *honu* – is regarded as a sign of good fortune, viewed as a sacred creature and symbol of spiritual energy. It represents spiritual guidance and the connection between sea, earth and human nature.

Tortoiseshell Cat

Stories of tortoiseshell cats date back to ancient times, and many of the superstitions regarding them still abound today. In Ireland and Scotland, tortoiseshell cats are thought to bring their owners good fortune, and in the USA, where they are sometimes referred to as 'money cats', they bring wealth. In Japan, these cats are said to protect ships from bad storms, shipwrecks ... and even ghosts, with beloved pets often accompanying fishermen at sea.

Only one in 3000 tortoiseshell cats is male, their rarity leading the ancient Celts to believe it to be a good omen if a male tortoiseshell cat stayed in their home. Some people even believe that if you dream of a tortoiseshell cat, you'll be lucky in love.

White Heather

One of Scotland's most common flowers, heather is a perennial shrub that grows in abundance in the highlands. Typically purple, it also grows in a rare white variety. To find a sprig of white heather is considered very lucky, just like finding a four-leaf clover. It is hung in the home to protect against fire, hunger and evil, and is sometimes still found in bridal bouquets today.

White heather's inherent luck was popularised by Queen Victoria, who held Scottish lore in high regard. In 1884 she wrote about her servant collecting a sprig while on a trip to Scotland. Such was Queen Victoria's esteem for these superstitions that she even named her pet Angora cat White Heather.

Wishbone

The ancient Etruscans, living around 700 BCE, believed that chickens had a mystical connection to the future. The forked wishbone – the furcula – of the chicken was dried out in the sun for several days before being kept in the home, where it was asked for favours and wishes by all who encountered it.

The Romans took this tradition and added a competitive edge: two people took hold of opposite sides of the wishbone, then pulled to break it in two while making a wish. Whoever held the bigger piece was said to have their wish granted. It is thought this is where the phrase 'to get a lucky break' stems from.

Wishing Well

The wishing well is thought to have originated in European folklore. With water a scarce and thus valuable resource, a well was viewed as a blessing from the gods. This gave rise to the belief that wishes spoken into a well would be granted. The wise Nordic god Mimir guarded a well, and according to legend drinking the water of this well gave the gift of wisdom.

Celts believed wells were sacred, and would often make offerings to the gods by tossing coins and jewellery into the well, hoping for their wishes to come true. This practice continues today: coins are thrown into wells and fountains in a familiar ritual that will grant wishes and bring a little extra luck.

Wreath

Representing eternity, the wreath has been used throughout the ages, its circular form found in almost every ancient culture. In Egypt, people wore wreaths of onions – the vegetable venerated as a symbol of eternal life – while the Vikings celebrated the winter solstice by making wreaths of holly and ivy, later setting them on fire in the hope of attracting the sun's attention.

In ancient Greece, the laurel wreath symbolised power and triumph, and the famous Christmas wreath represents longevity; made from evergreen branches, it is resilient and retains its leaves through winter. Hung on the door or window, a wreath is viewed as an invitation to the spirit of Christmas to enter the home and bring in good luck.

About the Author

Megan McKean is an Australian designer, author and illustrator with permanently itchy feet and a curiosity for superstitions and beliefs in different cultures.

A long-held fascination with the iconography of lucky symbols has led to collecting countless charms and souvenirs from her travels around the world.

Whether it's spotting a ladybird in the garden, or plucking a four-leaf clover, Megan looks for a little extra luck in the everyday.

For Joshua
So lucky to be loving you

Published in 2025 by Hardie Grant Books, an imprint of Hardie Grant Publishing

Hardie Grant Books (Melbourne)
Wurundjeri Country
Building 1, 658 Church Street
Richmond, Victoria 3121

Hardie Grant North America
2912 Telegraph Ave
Berkeley, California 94705

hardiegrant.com/books

Hardie Grant acknowledges the Traditional Owners of the Country on which we work, the Wurundjeri People of the Kulin Nation and the Gadigal People of the Eora Nation, and recognises their continuing connection to the land, waters and culture. We pay our respects to their Elders past and present.

A catalogue record for this book is available from the National Library of Australia

Lucky: Symbols of good fortune from around the world
ISBN 978 1 76145 094 5

10 9 8 7 6 5 4 3 2 1

Publisher: Tahlia Anderson
Head of Editorial: Jasmin Chua
Project Editor: Antonietta Anello
Editor: Eugenie Baulch
Creative Director: Kristin Thomas
Designer: Megan McKean
Head of Production: Todd Rechner
Production Controller: Jessica Harvie

Colour reproduction by Splitting Colour Studio
Printed in China by Leo Paper Products LTD.

The paper this book is printed on is from FSC®-certified forests and other sources. FSC® promotes environmentally responsible, socially beneficial and economically viable management of the world's forests.